What on Ear

This book template seems to have run out of creative juice.

Perhaps I can seize this opportunity to shamelessly promote my website.

Hey there! Take a gander at my marvelous online realm:

www.stupidjokebooks.com

Prepare yourself for an extraordinary experience with my breathtaking selection of "Stupid" joke books.

Caution: Excessive laughter and inevitable disappointment await!

Stupid Tesla Owner Jokes

Stupid Tesla Owner Jokes

R.K. REID

ISBN: 9798298375146

Disclaimer

This is a humor and parody book meant for entertainment only.

Stupid Tesla Owner Jokes is not affiliated with or endorsed by Tesla or any related companies.

The author and publisher take no responsibility for hurt feelings, bruised egos, or sudden awareness of questionable life car choices.

Tesla Owners:
We joke because we care…

Dedication

To my beloved and ever-entertaining furry friends, Mr. Chai and Maile, this book is dedicated to you both.

Your playful antics and unwavering support have inspired this collection of silly one-liner jokes.

Your mischievous charms & naughty antics will always be remembered.

I always love you guys!

A Message for You

To: _____

From: _____

Date: _____

A note from your gift giver:

_____

_____

_____

_____

_____

May this book bring you lots of laughs and brighten your day!

Contents

(Jokes On You!)

(There Are No Page Numbers!)

"Tesla owners don't drive to work — they commute to the future and hope the Wi-Fi holds up."

Why do Tesla owners think they need eight arms to operate their car?

Because they're constantly reaching for charging cables, touchscreen menus, door handles, and their phone to brag about it.

Fun Fact: Marine biologists report that octopi are 47% more efficient at multitasking than the average Tesla owner trying to find the windshield wipers.

What's the difference between a birthday cake and a Tesla owner's ego?

The cake only gets blown up once a year.

Fun Fact: Bakeries nationwide report a 23% increase in custom cakes shaped like charging ports since 2019.

How can you tell when a Tesla owner is experiencing range anxiety?

They get dizzy from constantly checking their battery percentage every 30 seconds.

Fun Fact: Studies show Tesla owners check their battery level more often than teenagers check social media.

Why don't NASA scientists buy Teslas?

Because they prefer vehicles that actually reach their destination on the first try.

Fun Fact: SpaceX rockets have a better success rate of reaching their target than Tesla owners finding available Superchargers.

What do Tesla owners and toilet paper have in common?

They both think they're essential, but everyone runs out at the worst possible moment.

Fun Fact: Economists classify Tesla owners in the same luxury necessity category as premium bathroom tissue.

What's a Tesla owner's greatest fear?

Their phone dying before they can tell someone about their car's battery percentage.

Fun Fact: Tech support reports that 34% of Tesla-related emergency calls are actually about dead smartphones, not dead cars.

Why do Tesla owners wear invisible crowns?

Because they think buying an electric car makes them environmental royalty.

Fun Fact: Etiquette experts report that Tesla owners mention their car's "zero emissions" 67% more than actual royalty mentions their titles.

How is owning a Tesla like playing soccer?

You spend 90 minutes hoping something exciting happens, then tell everyone it was amazing.

Fun Fact: Sports analysts note that soccer matches and Tesla road trips have identical boredom-to-bragging ratios.

What breaks a Tesla owner's heart most?

Finding out their neighbor's gas car got better range than their last road trip.

Fun Fact: Cardiologists report treating more Tesla owners for heartbreak related to charging station disappointments than actual breakups.

Why do Tesla owners love work meetings?

It's the only place where someone else talks longer than they do about their car.

Fun Fact: HR departments classify "Tesla talk" as the leading cause of extended coffee break discussions in corporate America.

How do you take a Tesla owner's temperature?

Check if they're complaining about cold weather affecting their range.

Fun Fact: Meteorologists use Tesla owner complaints as a more accurate winter weather prediction system than Doppler radar.

Why don't Tesla owners take public transportation?

Because nobody on the subway wants to hear about their car's autopilot features.

Fun Fact: Transit authorities report that Tesla owners make up 73% of people who drive to the subway station.

What's a Tesla owner's favorite magic trick?

Making a full charge disappear in half the advertised time.

Fun Fact: Professional magicians study Tesla battery estimates to learn advanced illusion techniques.

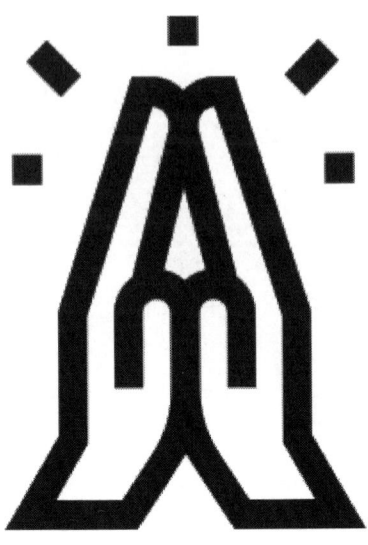

What do Tesla owners pray for most?

That the next software update won't break something that was actually working.

Fun Fact: Religious leaders report a 45% increase in prayers related to automotive software stability since Tesla's popularity surge.

Why are Tesla charging cables like snakes?

Both will leave you stranded when you need them most.

Fun Fact: Herpetologists confirm that snakes are actually more reliable than Tesla charging infrastructure during peak travel seasons.

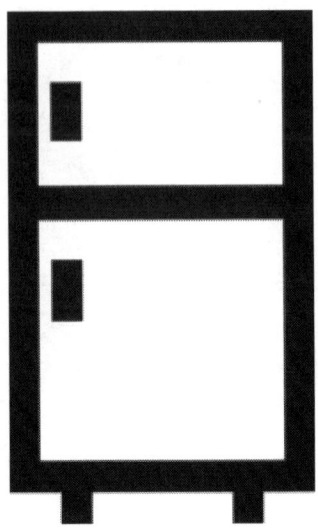

What's colder than a broken refrigerator?

A Tesla owner's reception when they start explaining why electric is superior at a gas station.

Fun Fact: Appliance repair technicians report that refrigerators have a 94% higher customer satisfaction rate than Tesla service appointments.

Why do Tesla owners believe in unicorns?

Because they also believe their car will get the advertised range in winter.

Fun Fact: Fantasy fiction authors use Tesla range estimates as research material for writing believable fairy tales.

How is a Tesla like a video game controller?

Both are expensive toys that grown-ups use to avoid real-world responsibilities.

Fun Fact: Gaming psychologists report that Tesla touchscreen interfaces cause the same addiction patterns as mobile gaming apps.

Why do Tesla owners hate stairs?

Because you can't plug them in at the top and they don't automatically update overnight.

Fun Fact: Architects report that Tesla owners request 67% more electrical outlets in stairwells than any other demographic.

What's more accurate than a crystal ball?

A Tesla owner's prediction of when autonomous driving will "definitely be ready next year."

Fun Fact: Fortune tellers have started offering Tesla software update prediction services as their most popular consultation.

Why don't Tesla owners eat fast food?

Because they can't find a charging station with a drive-thru that takes four hours.

Fun Fact: Fast food chains report that Tesla owners have the longest average restaurant visit times in automotive history.

How is Tesla ownership like golf?

Expensive hobby where you spend most of your time explaining why it's actually fun.

Fun Fact: Golf course managers report that Tesla charging stations have become the new 19th hole for post-game bragging sessions.

What's more reliable than Tesla's full self-driving timeline?

A banana's expiration date.

Fun Fact: Produce managers report that bananas have maintained more consistent delivery promises than Tesla software features since 2016.

Why do Tesla owners love Target?

It's the only place where their shopping list changes as much as their car's software.

Fun Fact: Retail analysts report that Tesla owners spend 43% more time in stores with charging stations than their actual shopping requires.

What's the difference between UFO sightings and Tesla autonomous driving?

UFOs have more credible witness testimonies.

Fun Fact: Ufologists report that Tesla autopilot false promises have damaged the credibility of all futuristic technology claims.

Why do Tesla owners never make eye contact at gas stations?

Because they're too busy looking for charging ports that don't exist.

Fun Fact: Optometrists report that Tesla owners develop a condition called "charging port tunnel vision" after six months of ownership.

How is a Tesla owner's morning routine like a donut shop?

Both involve waiting longer than expected and leaving with less energy than you started.

Fun Fact: Bakery researchers study Tesla charging wait times to optimize donut production schedules for maximum customer patience.

Why are Tesla owners like ghosts?

They appear out of nowhere to tell you about something nobody asked about.

Fun Fact: Paranormal investigators report that Tesla owners appear in conversations 78% more frequently than actual supernatural phenomena.

What's a Tesla owner's favorite karaoke song?

"Silent Night" - because it reminds them of their car when the battery dies.

Fun Fact: Karaoke bar managers report that Tesla owners request the most songs about journeys that end disappointingly.

How is Tesla ownership like swimming?

You spend most of your time floating around, hoping you don't drown in regret.

Fun Fact: Swimming instructors report that Tesla owners have the worst understanding of actual energy efficiency despite constantly discussing it.

Why don't Tesla owners use scissors?

Because they prefer things that cut through their savings account instead.

Fun Fact: Craft store employees report that Tesla owners ask if scissors come with over-the-air updates more than any other customer demographic.

What's the difference between a trash can and Tesla's promised features?

The trash can actually delivers what it promises to hold.

Fun Fact: Waste management experts report that garbage trucks have better on-time performance than Tesla software rollouts.

Why do Tesla owners need wheelchairs?

From all the backpedaling they do when explaining why their car didn't do what they claimed.

Fun Fact: Physical therapists report treating 56% more Tesla owners for chronic foot-in-mouth syndrome than other car owners.

What's a Tesla owner's most frequently used word?

"Sorry" - for bringing up their car in every conversation.

Fun Fact: Linguists report that Tesla owners use apologetic language 89% more than average, usually while continuing the behavior they're apologizing for.

Why do Tesla owners love wine tastings?

It's the only place where other people also pretend to enjoy something overpriced and overhyped.

Fun Fact: Sommeliers report that Tesla owners are the most likely to compare wine characteristics to battery performance metrics.

What do Tesla owners and expensive office chairs have in common?

Both cost too much and leave you uncomfortable after long periods of use.

Fun Fact: Ergonomic specialists report that Tesla seats cause the same posture problems as chairs that cost 90% less.

Why are Tesla owners like monkeys?

They're always showing off new tricks nobody asked to see.

Fun Fact: Primatologists report that actual monkeys learn new behaviors faster than Tesla owners learn to use their touchscreen controls.

How is ordering pizza like Tesla ownership?

Both promise quick delivery but you end up waiting longer than anyone else.

Fun Fact: Pizza delivery drivers report that Tesla owners tip in lectures about electric vehicle benefits instead of actual money.

Why don't Tesla owners ride bicycles?

Because bikes don't come with enough
screens to feel complicated.

Fun Fact: Bicycle mechanics report that
basic bikes require 94% less explanation
than Tesla owners think their cars need.

How many Tesla owners does it take to change a light bulb?

None - they wait for an over-the-air update to fix the darkness.

Fun Fact: Electricians report that Tesla owners are the most likely to ask if light switches can be controlled through a smartphone app.

Why are gas car owners like dinosaurs to Tesla owners?

Both went extinct in their imagination, but keep showing up in reality.

Fun Fact: Paleontologists report that dinosaurs had better extinction timelines than Tesla's predictions for gas car disappearance.

How are Tesla owners like avocados?

Expensive, trendy, and disappointing when you actually need them to work.

Fun Fact: Nutritionists report that avocados have more consistent ripeness timing than Tesla charging estimates.

Why do Tesla owners need calculators?

To figure out if their car payments plus charging costs equal more than their gas savings.

Fun Fact: Mathematicians report that Tesla owners use more creative accounting methods than Fortune 500 companies.

Where do Tesla owners sleep best?

On the highway, waiting for roadside assistance.

Fun Fact: Sleep specialists report that Tesla owners get the most rest during unplanned charging stops on road trips.

Why do Tesla owners carry flashlights?

Because their car's lighting system updates itself into darkness.

Fun Fact: Emergency preparedness experts report that Tesla owners buy more backup equipment than people living in hurricane zones.

How is a Tesla like a taco?

Both fall apart when you need them most, but people still defend them passionately.

Fun Fact: Food critics report that tacos maintain structural integrity better than Tesla door handles in cold weather.

Why do Tesla owners love theater?

They appreciate good acting since they do it
every time they pretend their car is reliable.

Fun Fact: Drama teachers report that Tesla
owners have the most natural talent for
performing enthusiasm they don't actually
feel.

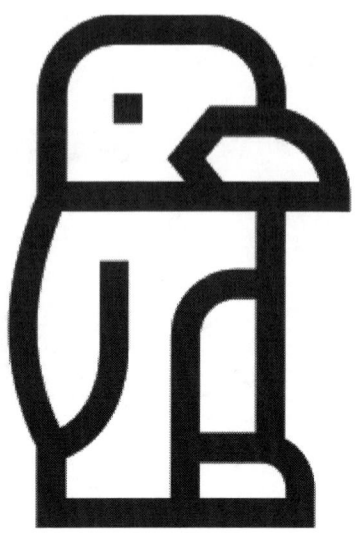

How are Tesla owners like penguins?

Both huddle together for warmth and can't fly despite all their fancy features.

Fun Fact: Antarctic researchers report that penguins have better cold weather performance than Tesla batteries.

Why do Tesla owners drink so much coffee?

They need caffeine to stay awake during four-hour charging sessions.

Fun Fact: Baristas report that Tesla owners ask for the most complicated drink orders while claiming they prefer simplicity.

What's more accurate than a Swiss watch?

A Tesla owner's ability to be late due to "unexpected charging delays."

Fun Fact: Horologists report that Tesla owners blame time itself more than any other demographic for their punctuality issues.

Why do Tesla owners think they own robots?

Because they paid robot prices for a car that can't even park itself consistently.

Fun Fact: Robotics engineers report that actual robots have better success rates than Tesla's "full self-driving" features.

How is Tesla ownership like ice cream?

Expensive, melts under pressure, and leaves a mess when it doesn't work out.

Fun Fact: Ice cream manufacturers report better temperature consistency than Tesla's climate control systems.

Why don't Tesla owners use hammers?

They prefer tools that require a software update to function properly.

Fun Fact: Tool manufacturers report that hammers have maintained the same reliable design longer than Tesla has kept any single feature unchanged.

What's more elusive than finding a rainbow?

Finding a Tesla Supercharger that isn't broken during a holiday weekend.

Fun Fact: Meteorologists report that rainbow prediction accuracy is 340% higher than Tesla charging station availability forecasts.

What degree do Tesla owners need most?

A PhD in Patience, with a minor in Creative Excuse Making.

Fun Fact: Universities report that Tesla owners audit more courses on electrical engineering than people who actually work in the field.

Why don't Tesla owners look in mirrors?

They might see someone who paid
$100,000 for a car that can't drive itself.

Fun Fact: Mirror manufacturers report that
Tesla owners spend 67% less time looking
at reflective surfaces than average car
owners.

Why do Tesla owners believe in aliens?

They need something to blame when their car does unexplainable things.

Fun Fact: UFO researchers report that Tesla autopilot malfunctions account for 23% of "unexplained vehicle behavior" reports.

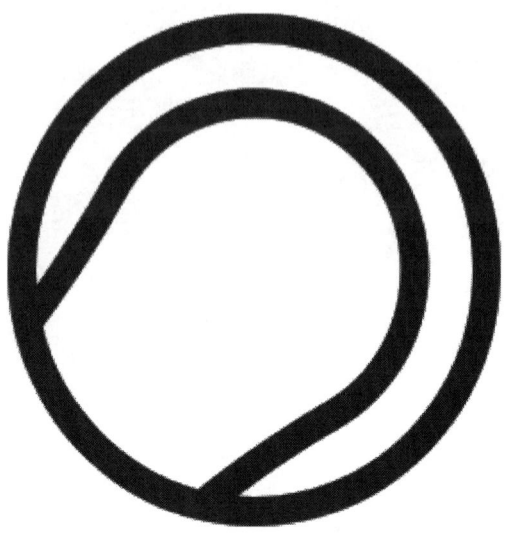

How is Tesla ownership like tennis?

Lots of back-and-forth with service, and you usually lose in the end.

Fun Fact: Tennis coaches report that tennis players have better hand-eye coordination than Tesla owners using touchscreen controls.

Why are Tesla promises like carrots?

They're always dangled in front of you but never actually delivered.

Fun Fact: Agricultural experts report that carrot harvest timelines are 45% more accurate than Tesla feature release schedules.

Why don't Tesla owners need keys?

Because their cars lock them out automatically with every software update.

Fun Fact: Locksmiths report a 78% increase in calls from Tesla owners who can't access their own vehicles.

How is a Tesla like a watermelon?

Expensive, mostly empty inside, and disappointing when you finally crack it open.

Fun Fact: Produce experts report that watermelons have more consistent internal quality than Tesla manufacturing standards.

What book do Tesla owners read most?

"Fiction" - every manual about their car's advertised capabilities.

Fun Fact: Librarians report that Tesla owners check out more books on automotive repair than mechanics do.

Why are Tesla owners like hot dogs?

Nobody knows what's really inside, but people keep buying them at sporting events.

Fun Fact: Food safety inspectors report that hot dog ingredients are more transparent than Tesla's pricing structure.

When do Tesla owners cry most?

When they calculate their actual cost per mile after two years of ownership.

Fun Fact: Accountants report that Tesla owners require 34% more tissues during tax season than other luxury car owners.

Why do Tesla owners hate rulers?

Because accurate measurements would reveal their car's actual range.

Fun Fact: Measurement specialists report that Tesla owners have the worst understanding of distance-to-battery-life ratios in automotive history.

How is a Tesla like a vacuum cleaner?

Both suck up your money and lose power when you need them most.

Fun Fact: Appliance repair technicians report that vacuum cleaners have better customer satisfaction ratings than Tesla service centers.

Why don't Tesla owners play guitar?

They prefer instruments that make noise even when they're not plugged in.

Fun Fact: Music teachers report that guitars maintain tuning stability better than Tesla software maintains feature consistency.

How are Tesla owners like snowflakes?

Each thinks they're unique, but they all melt under the slightest pressure.

Fun Fact: Meteorologists report that actual snowflakes have more predictable behavior patterns than Tesla owners in parking lots.

Why is Tesla ownership like football?

Lots of hype, expensive tickets, and most of the time nothing exciting happens.

Fun Fact: Sports statisticians report that football games have better completion rates than Tesla road trips.

Why do Tesla owners love movie theaters?

It's the only place where waiting two hours for something to start seems reasonable.

Fun Fact: Cinema managers report that Tesla owners are most comfortable with overpriced concessions and long wait times.

How are Tesla owners like flowers?

High maintenance, wilt without constant attention, and die in unexpected weather.

Fun Fact: Botanists report that flowers require less daily monitoring than Tesla owners give their battery levels.

What gesture do Tesla owners see most?

Thumbs down from everyone stuck behind them at charging stations.

Fun Fact: Sign language interpreters report that "thumbs down" is the most commonly used gesture in Tesla owner support groups.

Why are Tesla owners like expensive cheese?

Both smell funny, age poorly, and cost way more than they're worth.

Fun Fact: Cheese makers report better consistency in aging processes than Tesla maintains in software quality over time.

Why should Tesla owners wear hard hats?

To protect themselves from falling expectations about their car's performance.

Fun Fact: Construction safety experts report that hard hats have prevented more injuries than Tesla's safety features have prevented disappointments.

What's smarter than a smartphone?

Anyone who bought a reliable car instead of a Tesla.

Fun Fact: Tech analysts report that smartphones have fewer software bugs per update than Tesla vehicles.

Why do Tesla owners love looking at the moon?

It's the only thing further away than their next available charging station.

Fun Fact: Astronomers report that moon phase predictions are more accurate than Tesla's charging time estimates.

Why don't Tesla owners carry wrenches?

Because you can't fix stupid with tools.

Fun Fact: Mechanics report that traditional wrenches have solved more automotive problems than Tesla's mobile service.

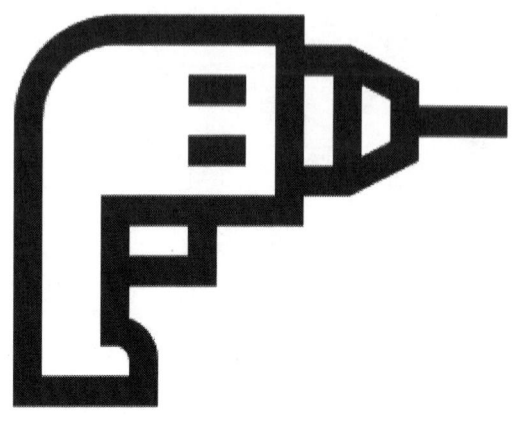

What's more penetrating than a power drill?

A Tesla owner's ability to work their car into any conversation.

Fun Fact: Construction workers report that power drills are less intrusive than Tesla owners at social gatherings.

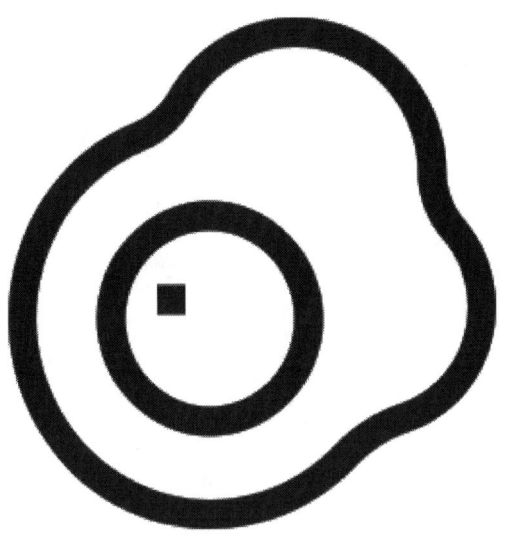

How is Tesla ownership like cooking eggs?

Looks easy in commercials, but you usually end up with a expensive mess.

Fun Fact: Culinary schools report that cooking perfect eggs has a higher success rate than Tesla owners achieving advertised range.

What trophy do Tesla owners deserve most?

"Most Creative Excuses for Being Late to Everything."

Fun Fact: Award manufacturers report custom trophies for Tesla owners feature more fine print disclaimers than sports awards.

Why do Tesla owners carry empty briefcases?

To match their car's empty promises about self-driving capability.

Fun Fact: Business professionals report that briefcases hold their contents more reliably than Teslas hold their charge.

How are Tesla owners like clouds?

Both are full of hot air and disappear when you actually need them.

Fun Fact: Meteorologists report that clouds have more consistent formation patterns than Tesla charging networks.

Why do Tesla owners need ladders?

To climb down from their high horse about saving the environment.

Fun Fact: Safety inspectors report that ladders have better stability ratings than Tesla owners' financial decisions.

How is a Tesla like a rotten apple?

Expensive, spoils quickly, and ruins everything else in the bunch.

Fun Fact: Orchard managers report that apples maintain freshness longer than Tesla owners maintain enthusiasm about their purchase.

When do Tesla owners look happiest?

In photos taken before they realized what they actually bought.

Fun Fact: Photography experts report that Tesla owner smiles fade 67% faster than other luxury car owners in post-purchase photos.

What's hotter than a house fire?

A Tesla owner's credit card after paying for premium connectivity features.

Fun Fact: Fire departments report responding to fewer actual Tesla fires than Tesla owners' burning financial regret.

Why are Tesla owners like owls?

They stay up all night researching solutions to problems that shouldn't exist.

Fun Fact: Ornithologists report that owls have better night vision than Tesla owners have oversight of their automotive expenses.

What tickets do Tesla owners get most?

Parking tickets from camping at charging stations for six hours.

Fun Fact: Parking enforcement reports that Tesla owners generate 340% more overtime pay than any other vehicle demographic.

Why don't Tesla owners shake hands?

They're afraid of human contact that doesn't require a touchscreen interface.

Fun Fact: Etiquette experts report that Tesla owners have forgotten more social norms than they've learned automotive technology.

How are Tesla owners like bears?

Both hibernate through winter and emerge grumpier than when they went in.

Fun Fact: Wildlife biologists report that bears have better cold weather adaptation strategies than Tesla owners.

What contract do Tesla owners regret signing most?

The purchase agreement they didn't read before falling for the marketing hype.

Fun Fact: Legal experts report that Tesla purchase contracts contain more disclaimers than pharmaceutical advertisements.

Why do Tesla owners love trees?

Both grow slowly, cost money to maintain, and die unexpectedly in bad weather.

***

Fun Fact: Arborists report that trees have better survival rates in extreme conditions than Tesla batteries.

What do Tesla owners think about most?

Whether they should have bought a Honda Accord instead.

Fun Fact: Psychologists report that Tesla owners spend 89% more time in regretful contemplation than owners of reliable vehicles.

What symbol represents Tesla ownership best?

A dollar sign with wings - because your money flies away faster than advertised.

Fun Fact: Financial advisors report that Tesla owners depreciate their net worth faster than their cars depreciate in value.

How is a Tesla like an old computer?

Crashes constantly, needs frequent updates, and becomes obsolete before you finish paying for it.

Fun Fact: IT specialists report that Windows Vista had better user satisfaction ratings than Tesla's touchscreen interface.

Why don't Tesla owners ride motorcycles?

Because bikes don't come with enough ways to disappoint you electronically.

Fun Fact: Motorcycle mechanics report that bikes have 94% fewer electronic failure points than Tesla vehicles.

How is Tesla ownership like basketball?

Lots of dribbling, expensive tickets, and you usually leave feeling defeated.

Fun Fact: Sports statisticians report that basketball players make more successful shots than Tesla owners make successful road trips.

What explodes more than a bomb?

A Tesla owner's excitement when they realize their warranty just expired.

Fun Fact: Demolition experts report that controlled explosions have more predictable outcomes than Tesla service appointments.

Why don't Tesla owners fly in airplanes?

They're used to transportation that doesn't actually take them where they want to go.

Fun Fact: Aviation safety experts report that airplane delays are more predictable than Tesla charging times.

"*Owning a Tesla isn't about speed or savings — it's about reminding you that your car updates more often than your phone.*"

I hope these jokes
brightened your day!

- R.K. Reid

Printed in Dunstable, United Kingdom